THE ISLAND OF ELBA

Written by
GIULIANO VALDES
in collaboration with
RICCARDO MAZZANTI

Photography
GIULIANO VALDES
G. BARONE

Published by
ITALCARDS
bologna Italy

Introduction

If nowadays the Island of Elba has become a tourist enigma, we shouldn't forget that its origins (as with all islands of a certain calibre) are steeped in myth. Legend has it, that along with its sister islands in the Tuscan archipelago, it fell from a jewel which adorned the neck of Venus. However we know for certain that Plinio il Vecchio described it as "insula vini ferax" in virtue of the excellent wines that were well known even in olden days. The great Virgil was fascinated by the richness of the minerals, and defined Elba as "insula inexhaustis generosa metallis". In more recent times, the island was chosen by Napoleone Bonaparte as a place on which to build his "golden" place of exile. He stayed here, in the shadow of his native Corsica for less than a year.

Generally speaking, Elba contains an immense quantity of landscapes, of delightful coves and enchanting glimpses of scenary, as well as an infinity of buildings which are of notable historic, artistic and architectural interest and therefore merits a very well planned and carefully thought- out itinerary. The pages which follow the notes on the geography and climate of Elba propose an itinerary of the island of Elba, and should help you in your "discovery" of the island, giving you useful suggestions and indications and thereby enabling you to construct a "picture" of the island which is both complete and yet at the same time vivacious.

This island which is a truelly green gem which emerges from the waters of the Tyrrhenian Sea never ceases to amaze us, because of its extraordinary qualities which help to construct a landscape painting which is dominated by the Mediterranean surroundings. Elba is a spectacle which continually changes, above all at the end of the summer, when, free from the grip of holiday makers and swept by the gusts of the Maestrale wind or by the first signs of the Tramontana wind, it reveals its inexhaustable beauty, offering the visitor the clearest and most luminous skies, the most gentle and attractive landscapes, the most brilliant colours and an endless silence which is broken only by the cry of the seagulls or by the pounding of the waves which break along the irregular coastline.

It is in the springtime when Elba is at its best. During this season the perfume of the broom, of the mimosa and of many other floral species permeate the slopes of the mountains and the rocky perpendicular coasts. The extraordinary vegetation is characterized by the typical Mediterranean scrub which alternates with the cultivated land. It should be remembered furthermore that as well as the presence of the characteristic maritime pine we can also find the holm-oak, the cork oak, the Indian fig and the agave. These species are in fact a telltale sign of an island climate which is exceptionally mild and benevolent throughout the year. From a naturalistic point of view the island has at least 150 species of minerals and numerous rocks from the famous porphyry, granite, tourmaline beryllium, h(a)ematite, magnetite and also quartz, schist, felspar, oligist and many other varieties.

1

2

The presence of this enormous mass of ferrous material also explains why there have been a lot of shipwrecks off the island and especially off Capo Calamita. These occurred because of the effect that the minerals of Elba had on the needles of the ships' compasses and the attraction between the minerals and the metallic parts of the ships. Whether this fact contributed to the creation of the "myth" that surrounds the island, we cannot say. However we know that on the sea-bed around the coast of Elba a great number of shipwrecks which occurred throughout the centuries have been found.

Finally we come to the history of the island: references will be made to it during the course of our itinerary. However we should like to briefly summarize here a few important points. The island was called "Aethalia" by the Ancient Greeks who started the exploitation of the metals. In Roman times it was known as "Ilva" (and this would explain the present name). In fact, the first inhabitants were the "Ilvates" a population from Liguria who established the first settlements on this island which is rich in minerals. These minerals were then exploited by the Etruscans in the furnaces in the nearby Populonia. During Medieval times, Elba, which was continually beseiged by the Saracen pirates, was controlled by Pisa, the powerful Maritime Republic, which left behind numerous traces of its domination, above all in the many defensive buildings and look-out posts. Following the defeat of the Pisan fleet in the Battle of Meloria (6-8-1284) the island briefly came under the control of Genoa. At the end of the XIV. century, Elba made up part of the State of Piombino, set up by the Appiani family (the princes of Pisa and Piombino). Later on the island was subjected to attempts amongst the powers of Europe (Spanish, French, English) to control it, and was also subjected to raids by the Saracen pirates. Finally under the control of the Medici family, its defence structures against the danger which the pirates presented were notably increased. In more recent times, Elba enjoyed its greatest noteriety when Napoleone stayed in exile here from 3-5-1814 to 26-2-1815. It then made up part of the Grand Duchy of Tuscany and then it became part of the Kingdom of Italy in 1860 with the restoration of the Congress of Vienna.

On the preceding pages: a view of the charming bay of Porto Azzurro. 1. Pine trees, the Mediterranean scrub and rocks characterize the Northern coast; 2. An aspect of the coastal morphology, 3. Coastal view towards Mount Grosso.

1

2

The island, geographical and climatic aspects

From a geomorphological standpoint Elba can be subdivided in three fundamental parts which are all clearly defined and characterized: the northern and southern have in fact an arrangement which is almost symmetrical with that of the main inlets, so that the main part of the island seems to be almost cut off from the rest of the island by two narrow "necks" in the longitudinal sense. Therefore the western part of the island seems to be separated from the middle by the isthmus formed by the gulf of Procchio in the north and by that of Campo in the south. The central part however is divided from the eastern part, corresponding with the "narrow" neck between the road-stead of Portoferraio and the gulf of Stella, with the adjacent gulf of Lacona. The separation of these singular geomorphological forms is accentuated by the fact that the two narrow parts of the island also correspond with an abasement of the reliefs which in both cases only arrives at a height of 50 metres.

1. Evening view of the gulf of Procchio towards Mount Capanne; 2. The roadstead of Portoferraio from the beach of St. Giovanni. On the apposite page: a panoramic view towards the gulf of Stella.

1

2

The western quadrant of Elba is characterized by the powerful granite formation of Mt. Capanne, 1019 m; from far away it seems like just one squat and compact block, with an elliptical base and with slopes that are relatively uniform, so as to seem like a big cone. In reality it seems to be incised by a great number of small valleys formed by the streams that run down along the slope. The summit takes on a particularly rough aspect and is covered by a series of steep rocky ridges. Numerous minor spurs come away from the central corps of the mountain, and these extend at a much lower, altitude towards the north (Mt. Giove) towards the south (Mt. Cenno) and towards the north-east (Mt. Perone). On the internal slope we find a series of small terraces (probably the remains of the ancient marine terraces) on which stand the centres of San Piero and Sant'Ilario in Campo. In any case one can see how the towns on the higher level are far more scarse, and all things considered, are also quite small. The rough and rocky nature of the relief of Mt. Capanne has always in fact acted as an obstacle to the setting up of any form of human settlement, and therefore Man has been forced to build along the coast, or else in areas which are not quite so steep. Because of this, and also because of several small streams which alleviate the summer droughts which inflict the whole island we find on the northern side the centres of Marciana and Poggio Terme. For this reason we can find in this area, woods and chestnut trees of immense size and which are certainly extremely old. Moreover the natural vegeta-

3

tion seems to be relatively scarse and greatly damaged by the summer fires which periodically destroy vast areas of the woods. On the slopes of Mt. Capanne, one can easily make out the distribution of the vegetation which varies according to the well defined altimetrical areas: in the lower part in fact, we find the classical Mediterranean scrub, consisting in the main part of aromatic evergreen shrubs like rosemary, myrtle, lentisk, the arbutus (or strawberry tree) and lavender. The Mediterranean shrub obviously alternates with the cultivated areas, at least where the slopes allow it to do so, with the presence of vines, olives, orchards and almond trees. On the southern side which is more exposed to the rays of the sun, the cultivated areas are often surrounded by Indian fig bushes and by dry stone walls which define the boundaries of the terraces. At a higher level and along the river valleys, the scrub gives way to the high forest trees like the holm oak and the cork oak, sometimes substituted in fact by the chestnut trees in the shady areas. On the highest

1. The pebbly shore of Capo d'Enfola. Mount Capanne in the background; 2. A view of Sant'Ilario in Campo; 3. A view of the coast towards Viticcio; 4. San Piero in Campo, the Church of St. Nicolò.

parts we find the conifers which were introduced by Man to create forests.

The central part of the island consists of a principal orographical junction, Mt. San Martino, on which two secondary mountainous ridges join up. All the reliefs are, however quite steep, because they consist mainly of rocks which are quite resistent to the action of erosive agents: we can find, in fact, green rocks and limestone in the eastern sector and porphyry and granite along the rest of the surface. The rest of the area is scarsely populated on the higher levels, whilst the settlements of the coastal areas are definitely expanding and these tend to be concentrated around the flat areas. Also in this area the great expanses of flatlands are concentrated, such as the plain of Portoferraio and that of Campo.

The eastern region of Elba is also subdivided into two sections by the deep gulf of Mola and by the flat and marshy plain which lies alongside it. It is almost certain that this obvious depression was once a huge marsh which was divided by an artificial canal that united the gulf of Stella with that of Mola: this waterway was practically the port of the Roman settlement of Capoliveri, at least until the 16th century. It is not by accident that the name Mola seems to refer back to the Latin *moles* which means "pier". In more recent times the marsh seems to have been filled up by rubble which was transported by small water courses that descend from the nearby hills and was then transformed into a plain. Also the promontory of Punta

On the opposite page: the abundant Mediterranean vegetation; 1. Portoferraio as seen from the ferry boat; 2. A view of Capoliveri.

1. *Some aspects of the Northern coast guarded over by the Castle of Volterraio;*
2. *Rural crops near Patresi.*

Calamita, to the south of this depression, would then have been, not so long ago, an island separated from the rest of Elba.

The north eastern quadrant of Elba consists of a mountainous layer which stretches from north to south with reliefs situated at an average height of under 500 meters. A little more isolated on a north western spur of the ridge stands Volterraio, a craggy steep peak on whose summit stands a castle of the same name. The summit of this small mountainous chain is characterized by a series of peaks, of cliffs and rocky landslides, which run along forming a kind of ridge which is extremely uneven and has an Alpine aspect. This conformation which is quite unique because of a relief which is of a "hilly" type and of average height, is due once again to the particular hardness of the metamorphic and magnetic rock (sandy schists, jasper, green rocks and scarse granite) which are incised and formed by erosions. Although it is not very high up, the relief has a hard and imposing aspect, also because it rises directly from the waters of the sea: almost all of the north eastern region of Elba has no plains and the relief falls onto the coast in a sharp and sudden manner. Of the two slopes the eastern one seems less

13

1

2

steep and irregular and therefore is more suitable for human settlement: all the main centres, can in fact, be found along the coast (Porto Azzurro, Rio Marina, Cavo) or on the small inland terraces (Rio nell'Elba). The characteristic stamp of the landscape is rendered in this case by the presence of rich and renowned iron deposits which stretch out endlessly, along the coast, starting from Porto Azzurro until Cavo, with the centre of the area being Rio Marina. The mineral excavations take up a great deal of the territory and are also visible from the sea, because of the reddish colour of the oxides. The vegetation, which has suffered a great deal due to the summer fires, has, alongside the classical and omnipresent Mediterranean scrub enriched by holm oaks and huge oak trees, large expanses which were once cultivated and which today have been converted into forests of maritime pine trees.

The climate of Elba is defined by the experts as mid-Mediterranean because of a dry period during the three or four months which go from May to August and because of a winter which is particularly mild and a summer which is not too hot. The extraordinary mildness of the Elba climate can be attributed to the form and to the structure which permit it (even in the innermost areas) to benefit from the favourable marine influences. The average annual temperatures of the island are around 16°C at Portoferraio; even the average temperature in the coldest month (January) maintains a relatively high level (around 10°C), whilst in the hottest month (July) they reach 25°C. In other centres of the island, including those at a higher level, no great variations in temperature have been recorded: the average temperature in the summer oscillates between 19 and 25° and in the winter between 6 and 10°. Even the absolute minimum temperatures rarely go under 0° (in January) and the maximum temperatures don't reach higher than 34-35°, thanks to the sea breezes and the slopes which cool the air during the hottest hours. The humidity of the air, thanks to the evaporation of the sea water contributes in maintaining the thermic valences within a certain range, not only the annual ones but also the daily ones too: the annual ones between January and July do not exceed 16° whilst the daily ones do not exceed 4,7° in December and 7,8° in August.

As to the precipitations it should be noted that the rainfall on the island of Elba is quite scarse, in fact only on the higher reliefs on the western part do the values reach 1000 mm per year, whilst along the coast these values are halved. Furthermore it is worth noting that the number of days which are completely serene is exceptionally high. The rainy days, by contrast, do not exceed a total of seventy throughout the year. Not only the rainfall, but also the number of days in which it rains tend naturally to be during the seasons of autumn and spring, whilst during the summer it would be quite unusual to get 55 mm of rain. Fog is relatively rare on the island because of the presence of sea winds and snow is very rarely seen here.

The climate of Elba is without doubt excellent for seaside tourism, which can count on marvellous weather even in the months which procede the summer (May-June) and even during the months which follow the summer (September-October).

1. Panorama of Rio Marina in the mining district; 2. Porto Azzurro, a view of the port; 3. Characteristic rocks along the Northern coast; 4. The Island of Elba as seen from Piombino.

1. *Porto Azzurro, an evocative panoramic view; 2. Porto Azzurro, a picturesque corner.*

Porto Azzurro

The small town has around 3,000 inhabitants and is set around an enchanting bay, open in the north by the deep, pleasant gulf of Mola. Porto Azzurro is the second port of call of the island, after Portoferraio. Frequent ferries secure the connections between it and Cavo and Piombino.

In 1947, the inhabitants tried to substitute the gloomy name of *Portolongone* (from an old Greek term which means "mooring stone") with the present name which in fact is more in keeping with the touristic notoriety which the place enjoys and which corresponds a little better with the pleasantness of the place. The original nucleus was developed on the adjacent hill beginning from 1603, when the Spanish monarch, Philip the third, ordered the building of the Fort of San Giacomo, which was to control the entry into the gulf of Mola, and the expansionist aims of the Grand Dukes of Tuscany on the island. With this loss of importance of Elba as a strategic point, its reassembling under the goverment of the Grand Duchy and with the end of bold pirate raids, the population abdoned this area close to the Fort (which was then transformed into a jail) and moved to the shores of the small cove at the base of the promotory, to carry out various activities such as fishermen etc: even today the population of Porto Azzurro is made up, in the greater part, of descendents of the Neapolitan immigrants, drawn to Elba, by this flourishing activity.

1

The most substantial part of this picturesque small town looks out over the bay, which in summer becomes a refuge for a great number of pleasure boats and has an almost vaguely exotic aspect because of the presence of agaves and Indian figs on the nearby cliffs and in the gardens of the villas. On summer evenings the *promenade* of the centre, illuminated by lamps and by the lights of the shops and by the ships moored along the quay, seems particularly romantic and elegant, to the extent that villagers and visitors from the nearby villages are drawn to it.

The presence of the Spanish in Porto Azzurro is backed by the beautiful small **church of Cuore Immacolato di Maria** which is alongside the *parish church*, and is characterized by the irregular plan, by the Spanish dome and by the belltower. Inside one can see the *monument dedicated to the General Diego d'Alarçon*, who also gave his name to the typical lanes of the historic centre onto which the church faces.

1. A glimpse of Porto Azzurro dominated by the Fort of San Giacomo; 2. Porto Azzurro, a view of the sea front; 3. Porto Azzurro, the small Church of Cuore Immacolato di Maria; 4. Porto Azzurro, the Parish Church.

2

3 4

But the element which is probably the most important from the tourist standpoint, and which is also linked to the Spanish domination is the **Fort of San Giacomo** which was built at the beginning of the XVII century by Philip the third, based on a plan by Don Garcia of Toledo, an expert in military architecture. For its construction, the citadel of Anversa was taken as a model, one of the most fortified and secure strongholds of its day. The fort stands on a promotory which slopes down, in a uniformed manner, towards the little gulf of Barbarossa (in memory of the famous Saracen pirate) and towards that of Port Azzurro; the mighty construction, which can't be reached from the sea because of the steep rocks, seems fortified by numerous ramparts and bastions, even on ground level. The central nucleus of the fortress has now become a *prison*; tourists can buy souvenirs that have been produced by the prisoners.

Another element which is characteristic of the small town is the airy and wide tree-lined square, which looks out onto the turquoise waters of the bay; in the many souvenir shops it's possible to buy metals which have been extracted from the sub-soil of Elba, or from foreign countries.

A view of the Fort of San Giacomo.

The Beach of Barbarossa

A little outside Porto Azzurro, there is a road which leads to this beautiful sandy shore which acts as a boundary for this evocative inlet which stretches from the Punta dello Stendardo to the Capo Bianco. All of this area is geared towards the tourist and tourist activities and there are many camp sites.

The wide stretch of sand is crowned by the blue waters of the promontory, over which the bastioned outline of the Fort of San Giacomo, also known as the *Fort of Longone* "reigns".

The coast under the fortress and the coast towards the Capo Bianco has a high, rocky conformation, whilst all around, a crown of bushes of the Mediterranean scrub can be seen, together with the Indian fig and verdant bushes of the maritime pine.

A view of the enchanting inlet facing the beach of Barbarossa

1

1. *The evocative position of the Sanctuary of Monserrato; 2. A picturesque view of the shore of Reale; 3. The beach and the mine of Terranera.*

The Sanctuary of Monserrato

This evocative building stands in a small valley, immediately under the steep slope of Mt. Castello; the steep, ruddy rocks help to confer an extremely strange and mysterious atmosphere on the landscape and the buildings, which are solitary and picturesque and seem to be "set" in the mountains.

The construction of the building, which was dedicated to St. Mary took place in the XVII century thanks to Pons y Leon, under the domination of Spain. The interior (which cannot be visited very often) has the venerable image of the *Black Madonna*, which is a copy of the Madonna of the same name which can be found in the sanctury which also bears the same name in the hinterland of Barcelona.

The Lake of Terranera

A little further on a branch of the main roads leads us to the **Beach of Reale**, which has a vast sandy shore in a pleasant position and within easy reach of the campsites. From the beach, an itinerary which is only possible on foot, takes us to the small lake of Terranera, and passing along the way an *abandoned mine* which bears the same name. Here the landscape has a particular aspect and is characterized by the fall of minerals which gives the characteristic black colouring to the shore. A thin sandy and pebbly strip of land, separates the small "mirror" of water from the sea. Seen from the top of the hill, along which runs the access road, its waters which are a dark green (because of the presence of a framework of natural vegetation and because of the mineral salts which are dissolved in the water) contribute, in contrast with the azzure waters of the sea, to the creation of a pleasant and fascinating chromatic effect. Its origins are artificial, due to the fact that it was formed after numerous and deep excavations for the extraction of ferrous minerals. Close to the north eastern margin which descends into the "mirror" of the lake with precipitous leaps and bounds, it is not unusual to find the bright cristals of *haematite* and *pyrite*. The presence of pyrite in the process of oxidation, provokes the formation of sulphereous incrostations of a yellowish colour around the surrounding rocks: until a few years ago, inside the mineralized mass, one could also see galleries which opened out, and through which a yellowish sulphureous water with a pervasive smell, flowed. The sulphur in this water was deposited on the bottom of the lake, and caused chemical reactions which made the water gradually hotter as it went downwards. This curious phenomenom has now stopped, but the waters conserve a strong therapeutic quality, and are used for treating illnesses of the skin, because small quantities of the sulphureous salts are always found in the lake.

2

3

3

Rio nell'Elba

Rio nell'Elba is a village which has around 1,000 inhabitants and is set on the eastern slopes of the mountainous ridge which spans, in a longitudinal sense, the higher portion of Elba. The natural position of the geographical spots acted as a catalyst for the establishment of towns in the olden days. The first inhabitants were attracted to this particularly secure place, because it was easily defended, because of the abundance of springs of water and because it was rich in ferrous deposits found in the subsoil.

Its name is probably derived from the latin *Rivus* = torrent, an allusion to the small water streams which lap the southern side of the town. In the XI century it was fortified by the Pisans, but the ramparts which they erected around the church were not enough to protect the town from the Saracen raids of the pirate Barbarossa, who in 1534, raided the place and destroyed it. It differs from the nearby villages of Grassula and Latrani (both

of which were also destroyed by the pirate), in so far as it was reconstructed after a very short period of time, and in fact, its population quickly grew because the survivors of the nearby towns which had been destroyed, decided to move to Rio nell'Elba. In modern times, the growth of the village has been accelerated by the establishment of its coastal "neighbour" Rio Marina which has become an important tourist and administrative centre. Today Rio nell'Erba suffers the highly negative influence of the crisis in the mineral sector which had always been the deciding factor in the economy of the place, as well as the abandoning of precious vines, destroyed by the disease of

1. A thin strip of sand separates the lake of Terranera from the sea; 2. A view of Rio nell'Elba; 3. The lake of Terranera.

1

2   *The oratory of SS. of the Trinity; 2. Rio nell'Elba, an aspect of the medieval nucleus; 3. Rio Marina, a typical view dominated by the Torrione Mediceo (Large Medici Tower).*

the vines and by the erosion which was unstoppable. In spite of this, the interest which the ancient mines holds, the evocative position of the lake and the boundless views towards the Canal of Piombino, towards the islands of Cerboli and Palmaiola and a wide stretch of the Maremma coast, have all contributed in reaffirming, in a positive way, the importance of the place from a tourist standpoint.

From an urbanistic standpoint, the village offers aspects which are decidedly Medieval, as can be seen from the narrow streets which look out onto the mighty constructions. The **parish church of Saints Giacomo and Quirico** has origins which date back to very remote times, even though obvious reconstructions are visible. At the time of the Appiani family domination, it was contained within the walls of a fort (XVIth century) which had been built to defend the town from the pirate raids.

The **Fortress** is a powerful quadrangular building, reinforced by ramparts at each corner. A little outside the town stands the **Oratory of SS. of the Trinity**.

In the immediate vicinity of Rio nell'Elba, one should note the small **church of St. Caterina**, a XVIIth century construction set on the southern slopes of Mt. Serra, in a district of particular archeological interest, and the crumbling ruins of the proto-Romanesque church dedicated to **S. Quirico**. Here there probably stood, up until the destruction of the building by the pirate, Barbarossa, in 1534, the settlement of Grassula, of which every trace has been lost. In the same area, *a tomb* has been found and which the experts believe could date back to the Roman period.

3

Rio Marina

The small town, which has around 2,500 inhabitants, faces a small bay on the eastern coast of Elba, which has been incised by the mouth of the river of Grassera. Opposite the small town, which is situated in the heart of the mining area, which was once extremely active, one comes across the small port which in the tourist season offers ''refuge'' to the nautical holidaymakers.

Up until the end of the XVIIIth century, Rio Marina was only a modest port of call where the ferrous materials dug out from the mines around the district were loaded onto ships to be sent across the world. The first human settlements were established in the course of the XIXth century, when the administrative offices of the mines were established. These attracted many inhabitants from the nearby village of Rio nell'Elba. In 1889 the birth of the autonomous Commune sanctioned, once and for all, the separation from the original borough.

The first impression one has of Rio Marina is that without doubt it is an extremely picturesque place: seen from the sea, the town can be seen to have the multicolour constructions which

seem to ''lean'' against the green slopes of the hill. The roads are narrow and dark, with the exception of the coastal road which leads to the port: immediately above the town the red and ochre small hills rise up, formed by the waste materials from the mines, which contrast with the greeness of the surrounding mountains and the blueness of a sea which is always deep and close by.

The most important tourist attraction is the **Torrione** (Large Tower) which stands near the pier, near extremely ancient buildings. The construction, with an hexagonal plan is surmounted by a look out tower, crowned by merlons, and probably erected by the Medici family (XVIth century) to defend this area of the coastline from the Barbaric raids.

In the *Town Hall* the interesting **mineralogical Museum of Elba** has been set out, where one can see in various showcases

the many species of the minerals which can be found on Elba. Even a visit to the *Mines* (which should be undertaken after having obtained a permit) holds a particularly naturalistic and mineralogical interest for the tourist. In fact the whole history of the Tyrrhenic island revolves around the vicissitudes of the mining comunity of this district. According to Diodoro Siculo the presence of a primitive iron industry can be proved by the name which the Greek navigators gave to the island, Aethalia = "spark", probably an illusion to the smoke and the fires which came out of the furnaces. This activity was taken up again and developed by the Etruscans, who starting from the VII B.C. took over the mines, taking the mineral (iron) to the nearby city of Populonia. The Romans, their successors, showed great interest in the mines, and actively exploited them, so much so that Strabone, went so far as to affirm that the mineral regenerated itself as soon as it was dug out of the ground. After the crisis of the Mediveal period, the exploitation was actively taken up by the Pisans, the Appiani family and the

Grand Dukes of Tuscany, but only came into its own in more recent times. In the last two centuries the progressive and intensive exploitation of the deposits brought about the complete exhaustion of these minerals. Added to this, the raise in mining costs has made the digging of these minerals become a completely uneconomic activity. However in the vicinity of Rio Marina, we can still see the yeards of long ago, inside which, it is not difficult to find the splendid crystals of haematite and pyrite which are the joy of naturalists and collectors. The long awaited realization of the planned *Mineralogical Park of the Island of Elba*, should guarantee a better safeguard and enjoyment of this interesting naturalistic patrimony.

Rio Marina, a characteristic aspect of the sea-front.

Minerals found on Elba: 1. Pyrite; 2. Ilvaite; 3. Quartz; 4. Granite; 5. Ilvaite; 6. Pyrite (Rio Marina).

29

1

1. *Cavo a view towards the Island of Mice and the canal of Piombino; 2. Cavo, a panoramic view; 3. Cavo, the pebbly shore of Capo Vita.*

The Tower of Giove

The tower, unfortunately left to ruin, rises up on the summit of Mt. Giove, directly above one of the most important mines for the extraction of ferrous minerls. The hand-built construction was built during the domination of the Appiani family (the second half of the XV century) and was for a long time, thought to be proof of an ancient temple dedicated to the divinity.

However we cannot exclude the fact that it might have been the spot where an ancient castle was constructed on the ruins of a pre-existing Roman or even pre-Roman settlement. It is easy to reach this spot by the scenic provincial road heading towards Cavo, which runs along the coast, through meadows and woods which offer beautiful panoramic views of the mines, of the Canal of Piombino and of the Tuscan mainland which faces the island of Elba.

Cavo

The spot is a quiet hamlet of Rio Marina and looks out on to a wide sickle-shaped bay, opposite the islands of *Palmaiola* and *Cerboli*. The beauty of the place is marked by the vast and extensive sandy shore, closed to the north by the small peninsular of Capo Castello. The blue turquoise water of the sea, gives a pleasant contrast to the greeness of the pines, which slope down from the surrounding hills to the Capo Castello.

Here, once upon a time, one could find the ancient *Cala Volbiana*, where the ships used to land as far back as ancient times: at this point, in fact, the distance between the dry land and this point is only eleven kilometeres. The name of the place seems to derive from the Latin *Cavus* = inlet or creek, or also *Caput* = promontory, refering to the small mountainous peninsular which stretches out towards the Canal of Piombino and fixes the boundaries of the gulf at the northern end. A marble plaque states that Garibaldi stayed here in 1849, briefly interupting his journey towards Caprera.

Near the Capo Castello one can find the ruins of the **Roman Villa of Faleria**, which are set in an area clearly marked by the presence of villas and tourist residences. In the vicinity the magnificent bay stretches from Capo Vita to Capo Castello. The extraordinary transparency of the waters, the stretch of pebbly and sandy shore, the reliefs covered with pines and Mediterranean scrub, which slope down towards the water, all constitute together with the *small island of "Topi"* to give a scenic and landscape picture of extraordinary evocativeness.

2

3

The Castel of Volterraio

The scenic route which from Rio nell'Elba arrives at Magazzini and then leads on to Portoferraio, crosses the ridge which makes up the framework of the eastern portion of the island, and allows one to admire the extremely vast and varied panorama over most of Elba: towards the west a marvellous view of the roadstead of Portoferraio opens out in all its entirety, the island of Capraia, Mt. Capanne and other strips of Mediterranean Sea can be seen. Towards the east one can look across a beautiful stretch of land which faces the Canal of Piombino, onto the small islands of the Canal and onto the Tuscan coast and the towns of Populonia and Punta Ala.

The gloomy Castel of Volterraio is visible from most parts of the island, and guards from high up the gulf of Bagnaia and the roadstead of Portoferraio. For the people who get to the island by means of the ferry, its sinister profile looks down threateningly from above the mountainous ridge.

It was constructed in the XIth century by Vanni di Gherardo Rau, during the period of the Pisan domination; it was to be a look-out post and a shelter from the Saracen raids. On the site probably even in Etruscan times, a settlement on a high altitude of the acropolis type which, legend has it, was dedicated to the mythological queen Ilva was found and from whose name the present name of *Elba* was derived. However there is no proof of this, except for the name of the locality: Volterraio could in fact refer to the city of Volterra which was probably the place from which the Etruscans came, and they established their colony here, or, maybe, it derives from the Latin = *Vultures*. Indeed, even now, the fort which has been built on inacessable rocky peaks, which break away laterally from the main chain of mountains, gives the impression of a "nest" for eagles or vultures, who guard the island and the surrounding sea.

The fortified structure is inserted into a landscape painting which is characterised by the lush Mediterranean scrub, enriched by the presence of the holm-oak which thrives along these mountainous slopes. The castle of Volterraio clearly shows its typology and its marked medieval characteristics: the ruins of what was the main bulk of the castel can be seen in the centre of a courtyard, surrounded by walls, whilst some structures are clearly visible, as for example, the main tower, the cistern used for gathering water, the Guard room and the sentry rounds.

An evocative view of the Castle of Volterraio.

Bagnaia

The town is a charming resort in the Commune of Portoferraio, and it looks out onto a picturesque bay which has its boundaries fixed by the Punta degli Scarpellini and by Punta Pina. The wide expanse of sandy and pebbly bay is surrounded by the hilly spurs which slope down to the sea, covered by green and balmy pines. The exceptional transparency of the sea water and the intense turquoise blue of the waters all combine to produce a picture of intense evocative surroundings.

Bagnaia and the nearby villages of **Nisporto** and **Nisportino** are in part overlooked by a great number of tourists and maybe this has been a positive fact in maintaining the tranquility of the place and for the beauty of the place. Even the last two towns look out over scenic coves which are open to the north, and have full tourist facilites including facilites for campers. The magnificent beaches, sometimes sandy, sometimes pebbly, opening out along the north eastern coast of Elba have extremely interesting morphological and naturalistic aspects.

1. Bagnaia, a panoramic view of the gulf; 2. Bagnaia, an aspect of the pebbly shore.

33

Magazzini

The pretty resort looks out onto the wide roadstead of Porto-ferraio in the south eastern part. A long and narrow sandy pebbly shore branches off from the small port, which during the "season" is literally beseiged by holiday makers and their boats. The views that one can see and which stretch out towards the main town of the region are exceptional, and the town is guarded by its fortifications and its port, and towards the north eastern coast there is an evocative succession of capes and coves cheered by the presence of the maritime pines, which in summer offer shade and shelter thanks to their thick foliage.

In the vicinity, in a village called *Ottone*, there are some interesting botanical gardens. **Villa delle Palme**, which contains numerous exotic species and reconfirms the extraordinary mildness of the insular climate of Elba. In the nearby hinterland stands the beautiful little church of **Santo Stefano alle Trane**, a precious jewel of Romanesque-Pisan architecture, which confirms the presence of the Maritime Republic from the XII to the XIII centuries. The building has a façade which is built of great square blocks of stone and is divided lengthwise by pilaster strips whilst a long series of small blind arcades decorate the building. The marvellous small rear apse is marked by a crown of small arches which jut out and in the centre of the apse we find a small window. Furher down along the slopes of the hill, a sequence of double coloums with Corinthian capitals makes the place even more evocative.

The church is in all probability the last testimony of the medieval village of *Latrani* which disappeared completely in 1534 after its destruction at the hands of the Saracen pirates.

The Roman Villa of Grotte

On the road for Portoferraio, at the same height as Punta delle Grotte, stands the substantial ruins of a big Roman villa of the Imperial, period. It is believed that its construction took place at the time of the Emperor Adriano, although other sources maintain that it belongs to a much earlier period between the I century B.C. and the first century A.D.

The interesting ruins stand in extremely evocative surroundings and allow one to admire, in its entirety, the roadstea of Portoferraio, dominated by the town, which looks like an island emerging from the Tyrrhenian waters in the cosy harmony of its constructions set in a semi-circle around the port.

The villa was discovered at the beginning of the 1960's and has many rooms, such as the huge *thermal swimming pool*, which shows the ingeneous technical devices created for heating the water, some *cisterns*, some *rooms* and structures *used as storehouses*, traces of a small *temple* and pieces of *mosaic ornaments*. A little further on a branching off of the road leads us to **Thermal Baths of S. Giovanni**. In this modern thermal building which stands on the site of ancient salt mines, the marine mud, rich in iodine and organic sulphur is used in the treatment of rheumatism and skin and bone disorders.

1. Magazzini, the tourist port; 2. The facade of the Church of Santo Stefano alle Trane; 3. The enchanting roadstead of Portoferraio which acts as a background to the ruins of the Roman Villa. 4. The Roman Villa of Grotte, the masonry in opus reticulatum.

Portoferraio

The town has around 11,000 inhabitants and is the major port of call for navigation and ships etc., as well as being the chief town of the island. The town has a particular importance from an administrative point of view and for the service sectors in general, having the role of polarisation, which extends along the whole of the island.

Portoferraio stretches out along the peninsular towards the roadstead of the same name, to the east of Punta di Capo Bianco. The area of the oldest urban settlements is set around the port and is surrounded by powerful fortifications which were built in the era of the Medicis.

All the historic centre offers aspects of considerable importance from an urbanistic point of view, with narrow lanes, open wide tree-lined piazzas, the town gates and the steep and almost inaccessible flights of steps. The top of the promontory on which the town is built is made up of two small reliefs which look out onto the high and steep coasts towards the open sea, and has banks which are smaller and more accessible towards the interior of the gulf.

From a military and a strategic point of view the topographical spot has been a decisive factor even from the times of the early settlements, having a rampart which is virtually impregnable from the outside, thanks to the narrowing at the base of the peninsular which makes up a really thin and small isthmus. However, once it was occupied the peninsular became an authentic advanced bridge head for the attempted penetration of the island, and was a thorn in the side of the enemy. It is not by accident that modern historians tend to identify this place with the ancient port of *Argoos*, which was remembered by the Greek navigators even back as far as the VIIth century B.C. Without doubt the Roman colony of *Fabricia* stood here, a port from which iron minerals were shipped. The presence of

this colony is confirmed by the discovery of archeological exhibits which are found in the waters of the roadstead. After the destruction carried out by the Longobards, the centre rose up again in Medieval times and was known as *Ferraia*, and then came under the control of the Pisans and then the Appiani family of Piombino. However the foundation of the present city can be attributed to the Grand Duke of Tuscany, Cosimo the first, of the Medici family, who, in 1548 ordered the formidable system of fortification, which today dominates the roadstead, to be built. It is thanks to the architects G.B. Camerini and G.B. Bellucci, also known as *San Marino* that the project and the realization of the new powerful city/fortress whose name *Cosmopolis* (the city of Cosimo, but this name also had the calculated ambiguity of "City of the Cosmos") was carried out, and this name testifies the expansionist aims of the Medici principality. In only eight months the superb defensive stongholds of Forte Falcone and Forte Stella were carried out, and immediately afterwards the defense of the dock with the construction of the coastal fortress of Linguella were also completed. Later on the defences were again strenghened with the construction of the ramparts of *Maggiore* and *Pagliai*, on the eastern front and that of *Mulini*, between Fort Stella and Fort Falcone. The western slope was reinforced, however by the construction of the so-called *Fronte d'Attaco* made up from

A detail of the ruins of the Roman Villa of Grotte (above). On the opposite page: Portoferraio, an evening view of the port.

Above: Portoferraio and the fortifications seen from the ferry boat.

Below: a view of Portoferraio and its port, dominated by the Medici forts.

Above: An evening view of the dock of Portoferraio dominated by Fort Falcone.

Below: An evening view of the dock of Portoferraio, with Porta a Mare in the background.

1

2

3

the ramparts of *Cannone* , of *Veneziano* , of *Palle di Sopra* and *di Sotto* and from the *Cornacchia* , and with the excavations of a canal which cut the isthmus between the roadstead and the open sea, protecting the side which faced inland. With this and other minor defensive structures, the city became almost impregnable as a fortress and retained its strategic role up until the beginning of the XIXth century. At the time of the Lorraine domination the present name of Portoferraio came into existence and port activities connected with the transporting of the iron minerals, the production of sea salt (the salt works of S. Rocco, of S. Giovanni, of S. Pietro and Ghiaie) and the tuna fish activities were all developed.

The city enjoyed its most splendid period under the brief Napoleonic administration in 1814, when it became the capital of a small kingdom, but was however the centre of attraction in Europe. At the end of this Napoleonic parenthesis, the city once again made up part of the Grand Duchy of Tuscany, and remained so until the unity of Italy. At the end of the XIXth century, the construction of the factory "The Blast Furnaces of Ilva" transformed the city into a centre of ironworks of national importance, bringing about a new period of prosperity which was interupted in 1943 with the destruction of the industrial plants, because of the air bombings. These were not rebuilt and today the economy of the centre thrives basically on the service sector activities (commercial, turistic and public administration activities).

From an urbanistic standpoint, Portoferraio has a bipolar order: in the east lies the ancient nucleus of the town, which is of pure XVIth century influence, arranged around the dock,

1. Portoferraio, the Linguella and the Tower of Martello; 2. Dawn over the beach of Ghiaie; 3. Boats moored at night in the dock of Portoferraio; 4. Portoferraio, the Porta a Mare

41

1. Portoferraio, the Parish Church; 2. The Church of Misericordia, the death mask of Napoleon Bonaparte; 3. The Church of Misericordia, a cast of the hand of Napoleon Bonaparte.

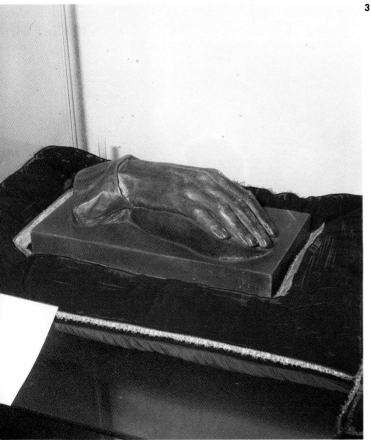

with a series of small streets that branch off and penetrate the older parts of the town. In the west we find groups of more recently built buildings which stretch out even as far as the industrial suburbs of Carpani.

The *dock*, which picturesquely dotted with ships of all kinds, is characterised by the XVIth century fortress of **Linguella** which has a star shaped plan and which makes up one of the Medici defense structures culminating in the massive octagonal brick structure of the **Tower of Martello**.

Through the mighty *Porta a Mare* (town gate) which was built within the Medici perimeter, and which has been partly transformed by alterations, one comes to the appropriately named historic centre. Beyond *Cavour Square*, which represents the most active nucleus of the old town the tree-lined *Piazza della Repubblica* opens out. Many interesting buildings face out onto this piazza: the **Parish Church** which was built in the first half of the XVIth century, at the time of Cosmo the first, and was later transformed. The **Town Hall** in which we can find the extremely well-furnished *Foresiana library*, the archeological exhibits, and epigraphical inscriptions in the courtyard. This building was once known as the *Biscuit Factory*. On the façade of the building there is an inscription which commemorates the presence of Bonaparte on the island.

In this area stands the **Church of Misericordia (**second half of the XVIth century) which is extremely interesting because of the Napoleonic memorabilia which is contained within, and especially for the copy of the *death mask* and a *hand* of the

Emperor himself, carried out by Antonmarchi. The church contains the keepsakes of Cristino the martyr, who is the patron saint of Portoferraio, and an exceptional XIVth century by Tino da Camaino, portraying the *Madonna and child*.

The nearby **church of SS. Sacramento** was also built in the XVIth century: inside we can admire some particularly interesting elements, amongst which stand out a painting on the ceiling carried out by Giovanni Camillo Sagrestani and figuring the *Assumption*.

The powerful **Fort Falcone** is a Medici work which was finished around the middle of the XVIth century. It has an irregular quadrilateral plan with three tenail walls and one rampart and is set in an area which is rich in defensive apparatus and service structures like the two magazines which are flanked by four curious lightening conductors in the shape of obelisks. From the glacises of the fort one can look out along the northern coast of the island and on to the opposite island called *Scoglietto* (meaning *Little rock*).

From the opposite side stands the powerful **Fort Stella** with its irregular plan of five points, inside which stands the so-called *Guards Quarters* and what was once the *Govenor's palace*. From the **Lighthouse** which dominates it and which was constructed in 1788, we can admire the view of the old town and of the entire roadstead with a marvellous natural port which

1. The Church of SS. Sacramento, a detail of the interior; 2. The Church of SS. Sacramento, the Assumption; 3. The Church of Misericordia, a Napoleonic banner with the Bees of Elba.

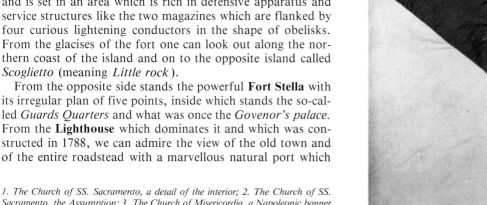
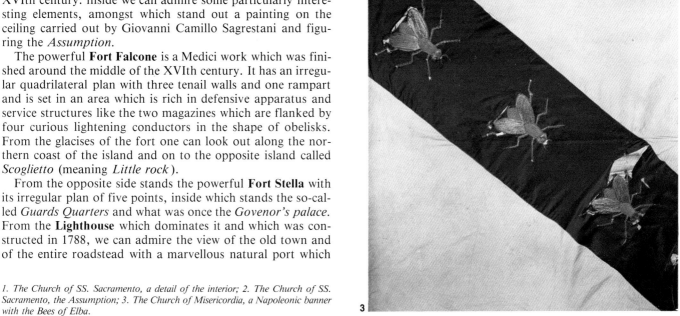

1

2

3

has been defined "as being, after that of Malta, the most beautiful port thanks to its vastness, to its depth to its security, that Nature has created on any of the islands in the Mediterranean".

Between the two fortifications is situated the so-called **Palace of the Mills** one of the two residences of Napoleon on Elba. The building, in which the Emperor and his retinue lived owes its strange name to some mills which stood here in the XVIth century and which were then transformed into residential buildings, from which the present construction has been built. Amongst the interesting rooms inside the building we should note, on the ground floor, the *Study, Napoleon's bedroom*, a *well furnished library* (containing over 1000 volumes given by the Emperor to the town) the *gallery*, the *reception room*, the *valets' room*, the *officers' room* and the *dressing room*. Some of these rooms stand out for the magnificence of the furnishings. On the upper floor one can visit the appartment of Paolina Borghese, Napoleon's sister. In one room note should be made of two busts depicting *Napoleon* and *his sister*. Behind the building is a beautiful *Italian garden*, decorated with sculptures and from which one can look out onto the fortifications of the city and onto the coast of Elba and the faraway town of Populonia.

Portoferraio is also an important seaside tourist resort; the tourist and the holiday makers can make use of the beautiful sandy shores of the *Ghiaie* (a sandy beach) of the *Paludella* (a pebbly beach) and the *Viste* (a rocky sandy beach).

1. Portoferraio, an evening view of Fort Falcone; 2. Portoferraio, Fort Falcone; 3. Portoferraio, Fort Stella; 4. Portoferraio, the Lighthouse by night.

4

1

2

1. Portoferraio, the Palace of the Mills; 2. Palace of the Mills, the bedchamber of Napoleon Bonaparte; 3. Palace of the Mills, Napoleon at St. Bernardo (J.L. David 1800).

3

The Napoleonic Villa of S. Martino

The interesting complex is situated inland from Portoferraio, at around six kilometers from the chief town, and it is easily reached by taking a small road which branches off from the main road leading to Procchio and which crosses the small green valley at the foot of S. Martino. Here in scenary of excpetional architectural and enviromental motifs, stands the elegant *Villa Demidoff* and the adjacent Napoleonic residence of S. Martino.

The rightly named Napoleonic villa which is also known as *Villa di S. Martino*, is in fact an unpretensious building which Bonaparte rebuilt from the restructurings of an ancient storenhouse, and made it into his summer residence, living there occasionally. The building has two floors; the rooms on the ground floor were used as service quarters, whilst on the first floor the rooms used by Napoleone and his retinue can be seen. The frescoes which adorn the appartment of Napoleone were carried out by Pietro Ravelli. Amongst the most interesting rooms one should note the *appartment of Marshal Bertrand*, the *Cabinet room*, also known as the *room of the Doves* because of the motif which decorates the ceiling; the *Egyptian room* which has motifs which refer back to Bonaparte's campaign in Egypt; the *Emperor's room* which is full of interesting furniture of the era, and the *Study*.

Coming out of the Villa one can admire the pleasant and luxuriant park which is dominated by the classical outline of the **Villa Demidoff**. This villa was built around the middle of the XIXth century by the Russian prince, Anatolio Demidoff, who entrusted the architect, Niccolò Matas with the project. The building has an air of great majesty probably thanks to the neoclassical façade. The vertical scan of the pilaster strips, the beautiful Doric pronaos with a triangular tympanum above it, and a classical frieze which has the motifs of the Imperial eagle, bees and the initial of Napoleone in capital letters.

These all contribute to show the building to better advantage, in an aesthetic sense, when the tourist sees it for the first time. The Russian prince, who was in fact a distant relative of the illustrious general, and who was an ardent admirer of the man, collected and kept in the Villa a great quantity of memorabilia, antiques and Napoleonic souvenirs, which were unfortunately lost in the second half of the last century. The Villa is interesting today because it is the seat of the **Foresiana Picture Gallery**, which holds a valuable collection of paintings, works of art and various objects, which date from the XVI to the XIXth centuries. The interior of the gallery which is architecturally extreme-

Palace of the Mills, a large hall inside the building (above). On the following page: the Neoclassical facade of the Villa Demidoff.

47

Above: The Villa of San Martino, the Egyptian Room.

Below: Villa Demidoff, the Gallery.

An old fisherman on the pier of Capo d'Enfola.

ley beautiful, is marked by a long series of solid coloumns which support a lacunar ceiling. In the centre of the room a marble sculpture of *Galatea* dominates the room, which was probably done by Antonio Canova who took Paolina, Napoleone's sister as his muse. Amongst the numerous paintings on view are the works of G. Fattori, T. Signorini, G. Reni, J.L. David, Borgognome (J. Courtois), G.B. Castiglione. The works on show here were collected by the nobleman of Elba Raffaello Foresi and then donated to the Communal Administration of Portoferraio which is in charge of the maintenance and upkeep of the place.

Again in the valley of San Martino, one can observe on the right slope some curious forms of erosion which look like furrows and characterise the clay soils: here in fact the water has dug out an infinity of small confluent canals inside the yellowish sands which have been mixed with slime, which can be found in abundance in this area. Nearby on the summit of a small hill, from which the roadstead of Portoferraio dominates, archeologica excavations on ancient elevated settlements are taking place, and here ceramic exhibits have been found which date back to the pre-Roman era.

Capo d'Enfola

One of the most interesting scenic excursions is that which goes from Portoferraio to the romantic Capo d'Enfola.
Going along a road which has many winding intervals, we get enchanting glimpses of the panorama. The waters which surround the promontory stand out because of their crystal clearness and for the sometimes sky-blue, sometimes turquoise colour. In front of the cape the outline of the rock known as the *Ship* which together with the *Scoglietto (Little rock)* make up an interesting spot which can be reached by either rubber dinghy or by ship.

The promontory which was also in origin a small island was afterwards joined to Elba by a flat, thin isthmus: in the most narrow part one can see, even today, the remains of the buildings of an ancient tuna-fish factory.

From Capo d'Enfola one can look out over the irregular northern coastline of the island, outlined in the background by the far away cliffs and rocks of Populonia. Towards the south the panorama takes in the pleasant gulf of Viticcio and the much wider gulf of Procchio, whose boundaries are fixed by the threatening characteristic outline of Mt. Capanne.

Two views of the extraordinarily transparent waters of Capo d'Enfola. On the following pages: an evocative panorama of Capo d'Enfola and its coasts.

A panoramic view of Marciana Marina, with the island of Capraia in the background. On the following page: views of the coast near Marciana Marina.

Marciana Marina

Along the itinerary that leads to Marciana Marina it is almost obligatory to make a small deviation so as to reach the pleasant towns of **Biodola** and **Scaglieri**. Both places have been blessed with a long and sandy front which slopes slowly and gently down towards a sea whose chromatic tonalities are always enchanting and intense, and where the hills which run down towards the sea form a scenic background, sometimes with high and rocky coasts, yet always covered with a green "conspiracy" of the typical Mediterranean scrub. The two centres are famed as being the most frequented seaside resorts on Elba and have modern tourist facilities.

The coastal road for Marciana Marina offers us intense and evocative glimpses of beautiful views which stretch from the pleasant gulfs of Procchio, of Biodola and Viticcio, as well as towards the characteristic outline of Capo d'Enfola which seems to fix the boundaries for the horizon of the coast.

One extremely pleasant and intense view is that which allows us, near the Punta Sprizze, to admire the picturesque small *island of Paolina*, which rises up in the waters of the gulf of Procchio, bringing down through history the memory of Bonaparte's stay on the island.

Marciana Marina is an enchanting centre with almost 2,000 inhabitants and looks out onto the pleasant coastline which is set in a semicircle and dominated by the powerful granite glacises of Mt. Capanne. Its importance as a tourist town is due to the beautiful pebbly shore of *Cala Fenicia* and due to the small port which in the holiday season is literally overrun by pleasure boats of all kinds.

The oldest nucleus of the place goes back to the XVIIIth century and is the locality called *Cotone* (from *coto* which means stone/pebble in the local dialect). Originally the small town consisted of a few fishermen's houses, many of whom came from Naples or Genoa. It was only later, after the drainage of the narrow coastal plain that the town was able to expand along the beach and up the river valleys of Marciana and San Giovanni. The new coastal centre is expanding and has attracted many of the inhabitants from the neighbouring mountain regions. So much so that in 1884 the new Commune of Marciana Marina was set up with lands separated from the Commune of Marciana.

55

Above: a panoramic view of the coast towards Biodola and Scaglieri.   *Below: The shore of Biodola.*

Above: Scaglieri, a view of the shore.

Below: dense vegetation surrounds the houses of Scaglieri which looks out over the beach.

Above: an evocative image of the Island of Paolina in the gulf of Procchio.   *Below: Marciana Marina, the pebbly shore of Cala Fenicia.*

1

The character of the centre is the exact opposite of the other communes of the island, because of its recent origins and the much more recent development of the urban area which has meant the construction of relatively large roads and squares, leaving no space for the typical forms of Medieval building. The only architectural element of historical value is the conic **Saraceno Tower** otherwise known as the *Medicean* tower which dominates the waterfront of the port. To tell the truth, in spite of its name, the construction dates back to the time of the Pisan domination and was built by the Marine Republic which had planned to use it to protect a landing place from the pirate raids which in those times was used along this piece of coastline. Today the Commune of Marciana Marina is counted as being amongst the most renowned wine growing areas of the whole island. The terraced slopes which reach high up the valleys towards Poggio and Marciana are thickly and densely planted with vines, which make up one of the well known characteristics of the landscape of this area. Here we find excellent red and white wines which are produced thanks to carefully specialized techniques which are still practised throughout Elba.

2

1. Marciana Marina, a view of the dock and the sea-front; 2. Marciana Marina, the Saraceno Tower; 3. Aspect of the coast near Marciana Marina; 4. Marciana Marina, a panoramic view of the pier.

3

4

1

Poggio

The village known also as *Poggio Terme* is situated in a pleasant and healthy spot on a granite cliff surrounded by thick and
shady woods of chestnut trees and holm oaks, oak and alder
trees. Also in this case the Medieval origins of the village can be
seen by its structure characterized by narrow and winding streets and by buildings which were built very close together as a
defensive ploy. The name *Terme* is linked to the famous fountain of Napoleone where, according to legend, the Emperor was
cured of gastric troubles which afflicted him and which even
today supplies the whole island with mineral water.

In the village we can find the ancient **church of S. Nicolò**
which is Romanesque in origin and which was built on the site
of a pre-existant fortified structure. Poggio offers spectacular
scenic views which on a clear day reach as far as Corsica, Capraia and even to the far away Gorgona.

2

1. Poggio, a panoramic view; 2. Poggio, the fountain of Napoleon.

Mount Capanne

In the district of Marciana some footpaths of interest to excursionists lead us to Mt. Perone and Mt. Capanne. The latter which is only accessible by cable car (the terminus is situated a little outside the town of Marciana) has been defined as the "roof" of the Tuscan archipelago. From the summit (1019 m) one can admire just as one could from an aeroplane, a great part of the coastal perimetre of the island of Elba, and we can furthermore look out as far as Corsica, the Tuscan mainland and the entire archipelago. The western side of Mt. Capanne can be seen in all its wild and unpolluted beauty thanks to the panoramic road which runs for the most part halfway along the coast. From this privileged position the seashore appears to be generally high and steep with brief promontories falling verti-

cally into the blue water. A series of small secondary roads which are narrow and winding, and some steep and inaccessible paths take one down to the beaches and to the small coves formed by the numerous water courses which descend from the main summit and here run into the sea.

Panorama of Marciana at the foot of Mount Capanne. On the following page: Marciana, a picturesque corner.

Marciana

This small town which has around 2,500 inhabitants is set in extremely pleasant surroundings on a ridge which slopes half way down to the coast from the powerful granite mass of Mt. Capanne. The characteristic small town is an important example of the medieval town plan and is surrounded by the green, relaxed countryside, where, the rows of vines and the shady foliage of chestnut trees can be found. In the district the *Costarella* wine, which is particularly praised by the experts can be found.

As the place name suggests, which is probably derived from the Latin *Marcius*, Marciana can certainly boast Roman origins; it seems in fact that already in 35 B.C. a Roman colony was built here. In medieval times the presence of an Appiani residence can be backed up by documents which date back to 1290. With the passing of time, however, its importance has radically decreased because of the birth and progressive development of the nearby centre of Marciana Marina.

The most important piece of architecture is the **Castle of the Appiani family**, which is a powerful turreted bulwark, which unfortunately today is completely ruined. The presence of the Appiani family can also be seen by their *house* which was built between the XIV-XVth centuries and by the *Mint* where money was printed. Amongst the other spots of tourist interest we should mention the **Antiquarium** where documents and material can be found which range from the Prehistoric to the Roman times and some *gates* which are built into the old **town walls**.

The outskirts of Marciana present spots of great tourist inte-

Marciana, two views of the Castle of the Appiani family.

Above: Marciana, a view of the bastions of the Castle of the Appiani family.

Below: the ruins of the Church of San Lorenzo. On the facing page: panorama of the gulf of Procchio and the Island of Paolina

rest. Along the road that joins Marciana to the homonyous marina stands the **Church of San Lorenzo** which was partly destroyed by the Saracen pirate, Kara Mustafà in 1553 and which unfortunately is in a state of abandon in the midst of the thick vegetation. This is a beautiful example of a religious building in Romanesque style, where the notable Pisan influence is immediately clear; in fact this church like many other parich churches of the island was built around the XIIth century, at the height of the Pisan domination (XIth to the XIVth centuries). The church has an almost rectangular plan and has one nave and three entrances: the principal door in the façade, opens out on the northern side; the two secondary doors face east and west respectively. The perimeter walls are made of small square blocks of granite, whilst the rear apse in in granite up as far as the impost of the arch and the cupola is made of tufa and limestone. The external part of the apse is enriched by an elegant crown of small blind arcades and small pilaster strips which show the connection between this church and the Pisan artistic influence. Higher up, in the centre of the façade, stand two pillars, probably the remains of a thin slender belltower.

On the northern slopes of Mt. Giove, in a district which has proved to be rich in interesting archeological exhibits, stands the **Sanctuary of the Madonna del Monte**, a spot where frequent pilgrimiges are made, especially during the festival of Mariana on the 15th of August. The building which was enlarged and restructured towards the end of the XVIth century holds a valuable XVth century *Madonna*, which was depicted on a granite slab. Nearby stands a small hermitage where Bonaparte stayed briefly during the summer of 1814.

The seaside resort of **Procchio** looks out onto the splendid gulf which bears the same name and whose profile is characterized by small promontories and projections, inside which open out evocative little coves of undescribable beauty. The magnificent sandy shore is counted as being one of the most attractive beaches in the entire territory of the Commune. The charming inlet seems to be crowned by hills of luxuriant vegetation by rocks and by islands like the aformentione *d'island of Paolina*, and by splendid villas in classic and modern style.

The south-western coast

This itinerary which starts out from Marciana goes along some parts of Elba that are not so well known but are however extremely evocative from a scenic and enviromental standpoint. The road, which has many winding bends should be driven along with great care, as for that matter all the roads on Elba, which are generally narrow and full of bends and curves. From the Commune of Marciana we reach Campo nell'Elba, by going along the whole circumferance of Mt. Capanne, which seems to peep out at every bend.

Numerous small branches off the main road enable one to reach the coastal hamlets which attract many seaside tourists, fishermen and pleasure boats and are characterized by a decidedly Mediterranean enviroment. From the sunny moors the characteristic rocky spurs rise up, whilst the coast, which is always high and steep falls straight into the sea, in a frame of wild and undominable beauty. The thick and luxuriant Mediterranean vegetation alternates with the ever present vines, whilst the agave and the Indian fig trees confer an exotic aspect on the countryside, heigtened by endless silence which is only broken by the cry of the seagulls and the pounding of the waves along the shores.

We pass the signs for *S. Andrea e Zanca* and cross the hamlets which make up the scattered quarter of Patresi. This area is thickly covered with vineyards which, unfortunately are threatened by the abandoning of the area by the inhabitants and the ever increasing number of houses which are continually being built. On a particularly clear day the view towards Corsica at sunset is extremely enchanting: it is maybe for this reason that the road that runs along the western side of Mt. Capanne is known as the *Road of the Sun*.

Halfway along the route we come to **Chiessi**, a charming village lapped by the waters of the sea which in this spot is of an extremely intensive blue colour. The pretty little cottages are surrounded by the green pines, and go back up along the terraced vine slopes, on which the rocky outline of Mt. Capanne stands. A little further on we come to **Pomonte** (whose

name gets its origins from the Latin expression *Post Montem*) a small group of houses which stands at the mouth of the valley bearing the same name, along a coast which offers the tourist spectacular views thanks to the presence of huge formations of roundish rocks which drop straight down to the sea in a chromatic contrast of great effect.

Along the southern coast, where we can look out onto the flat island of Pianosa, we come across the little town of **Fetovaia**. The most characteristic tourist attraction is the splendid sickle-shaped inlet which faces the narrow bay, whose boundaries are governed by the Punta di Fetovia. The wide expanse of sandy shore, beautifully crowned by pine trees, the long promontory which stretches out into the sea with its huge and rocky banks, the extraordinary transparency of the waters which are even today unpolluted and inviting, all make up an "oasis" of remarkably enchanting beauty.

We continue along the route as far as **Seccheto**, whose houses face out onto a little cove which has a small stretch of sand, flanked by rocks in front of it. The villas and residences are immersed in the green and shady "umbrella" of a thick pine forest and the small centre, like others along this part of the coast, is a much frequented tourist spot.
The ancient granite quarries are full of historical interest: it was from here that the materials used in the construction of the *Cathedral* of Pisa and the *Basilica of S. Paolo Extra Moenia* of Rome were taken. The surrounding territory is particularly well known for its excellent wines.

Nearby stands **Cavoli** which faces a small inlet, surrounded by the green pines and bordered by a beautiful sandy beach. The sandy shore of Cavoli seems particularly enchanting when seen from above the cliff along which the road runs: the various shades of blue in the water which change according to the depth and the nature of the sea-bed, form a contarst with the grey granite rocks of the coast, the silvery green of the luxuriant Indian fig bushes and the reddish purple of the bouganvillea. Far out to sea we can see the flat outline of the island of Pianosa and the frustum/conical outline of the mysterious and fascinating island of Montecristo.

A panoramic view of Chiessi (above). On the facing page: landscape views at Pomonte with its steep cliffs. On the following page: the marvellous shore of Fetovaia.

Above: Cavoli, a panoramic view.

Below: the houses of Seccheto stand out amidst a dense pine forest.

Campo nell'Elba

This highly populated Commune has around 4,000 inhabitants and is comprised of a large number of small houses grouped together and stands in the central-southern part of the island. **Marina di Campo** is without doubt the most important tourist spot, not only as a bathing resort but also as a resort for pleasure boats. It is a magnificently set out facing the gulf of the same name and is surrounded in the west by a series of hills and reliefs which stretch up as far as the summits of Mt. Capanne, which eventually give way to a vast plain, beyond which a series of hills separates the Elban side of Campo from that of Procchio and Portoferraio.

The natural roadstead of Marina di Campo is one of the most beautiful of the whole island and is a marvellous "shelter" for the boats. The pretty port which faces the town is still used by fishermen and pleasure boats often moor here; in summer it becomes transformed into one long expanse of rubber dinghies

boats and motor boats. The wide large sickle-shaped shore is bordered by a green pine forest, where many camp sites can be founds. The attractive, pretty centre of the town is equipped for tourists, and has many exclusive boutiques and shops, where the traditional souvenirs and artisan objects are on sale.

As a town, Marina di Campo is relatively new: even in 1870, where today stands the main part, only a votive chapel and the **Medicean look out tower** (XVIth century) stood. The latter,

On the facing page: the picturesque inlet of Cavoli, the Punta di Fetovaia in the background. A view of the port and the shore of Marina di Campo (above).

Above: a panoramic view of the gulf of Campo.

Below: Marina di Campo in the sunset.

Above: Marina di Campo, the sea-front.

Below: Marina di Campo, a view of the shore.

1

today dominates the port and some believe it dates back to the Pisan domination. The nucleus of the most ancient settlement grew up around the promontory which guards the gulf. On this site, the port authority buildings were also set up, and these soon became important for the sardine and anchovy fishing industries. The place also gained importance as the place from which the agricultural produce from the plain of Campo were shipped (this plain being the largest of the island). Today it is famous as a tourist spot. The area in which most of the new building work has taken place is the area along the main road which leads to *Pila*, where there is a little airport, which is mainly used by small light aircraft, although it has connections for all the regular scheduled flights from the mainland and even with some foreign airports, especially during the high season.

S. Piero in Campo is set in a splendid panoramic position, on a terraced slope which dominated the gulf of Campo. The town was probably founded by the Romans at the time of Octavian Notwithstanding the repeated destruction carried out by the pirates in both medieval and modern times, it has managed to conserve an urban structure which still re-echoes the original

Roman plan. After 1,000 the Pisans built towers and bastions, which were either destroyed or restructured, and these were built to defend the nearby granite quarries: the majority of the roads and walls of the town are still today built from this precious stone, so that the houses which are not whitewashed, seem to be built into the living rock.

The main tourist attraction, apart from the characteristic houses built in the medieval style, is the **Church of S. Niccolò**. This is a jewel of Romanesque-Pisan architecture and stands inside the dilapitated *Fortress of the Appiani*. It was partly con-

1. Marina di Campo, the Medicean look out Tower; 2. S. Piero in Campo, a characteristic small square; 3. S. Piero in Campo, a bastion of the Fortress of the Appiani family; 4. S. Piero in Campo, the bell-tower of the Parish Church.

2

3 4

1

structed on the site of a pagan temple dedicated to Glaucus, and its interior is divided into two aisles of equal width with round arches supported by coloumns. The capitals, which have a rustic apperance, re-echo the motifs of a decidedly archaic type, with strange *"monsters"*, floral decorations and artistic fantasies. Valuable XIV-XVth century frescoes, amongst which one of *San Sebastian*, one of *San Michele weighing the Souls*, an *Angel* and a *Saint* adorn the walls.

S. Ilario in Campo, in its structure and layout resembles S. Piero; pleasantly set in a sunny position, along the slopes of the western part of Mt. Capanne, and is full of pure medieval configurations. The houses which are white and blinding stand out amongst the vegetation and the terraced orchards, which have been patiently levelled out from the impervious slopes.

Even this small town has, probably Roman origins: its existence is backed by documents which however only go back as far as the Longobard period (715). The belltower of the church is the only sign left of the town walls built by the Pisans around the XIth century. It seems, in fact, that the **Church** was probably built by the Appiani family, inside an ancient castle. It once had only one nave, but at the end of the XVIth century two more were added: today it has a beautiful façade in the Baroque style.

This part of the island of Elba is extremely interesting from a mineralogical standpoint and has revealed valuable minerals such as the *pink tormaline* and *polychrome, granite* and *acqua-marine*. These minerals, in the past, were extracted from the quarry half way between the two centres named above. Only some discharges, which are often covered with weeds remain today, where sometimes collectors can, with great difficulty, find some interesting specimens. In any case, to protect the area from the excessive excavations and to protect the historic and naturalisti patrimony of the south western stretch of Mt. Capanne, it has been proposed that an institution such as a natural reserve be set up, which, given the lithological characteristic of these places, will probably be called *Granite Park*.

1. S. Ilario in Campo, the Parish Church; 2. S. Ilario in Campo, a panoramic view; 3. S. Ilario in Campo, a typical street in the centre of the small town; 4. S. Ilario in Campo, the church square; 5. S. Ilario in Campo, the bell-tower of the Parish Church.

2 3

4 5

The Tower and Church of St. Giovanni

Our itinerary now goes upwards, bracing the steep bends which run along the south western slopes of Mt. Perone along a route which is very popular with tourists and which allows us to go across the hills of the slopes of Poggio and Marciana.

The *Tower of S. Giovanni* is a mighty structure built on a quadrilateral plan and rises up on the summit of a colossal isolated granite rock. This fortification was built by the Marine Republic of Pisa between the XI and the XII century, and today lies in ruins along the top of the summit. The tower was origi-

nally used as a look-out post, to guard against the enemy which tried to attack the island from the sea (Saracens and Genovese) but it also acted as a last desperate refuge from the raids inflicted on the towns below it. It has only one entrance, on the northern side, which is more than two metres from the ground. One can reasonably assume that to get inside the building a ladder, which was then pulled back up to guarantee further security was used.

A little further along, unfortunately in surroundings which

1

3

2

On the facing page: the Tower of St. Giovanni; 1. The Church of St. Giovanni: a view of the interior (which has no roof); 2. The Church of St. Giovanni: a view of the apse; 3. The Church of St. Giovanni: a view of the facade surmounted by a bell-tower.

have been left abandoned, in the midst of luxuriant vegetation which makes it difficult to see, stands the *Church of S. Giovanni*, one of the most valuable examples of Palaeo-christian architecture on the island. It is commonly thought that it was founded before the IVth century, even if the structure which remains (and which has no roof) shows Romanesque traits of the XIIth century, which link it to the many other Pisan parich churches of the period. The interior of the church is particularly evocative, without its roof and pavements, surmounted by a pretty belltower which rises up from the façade whilst the apse has a small window and is characterized by a precious semicircular minor apse.

Further along the road leads to the large square of Mt. Perone, situated in the thick scrub which includes chestnut trees, pines, holm-oaks and mimosa trees. The views that one sees from here are indescribably beautiful. On a clear spring day one can see out along the whole island, and as far as the other islands in the archipelago and towards the Tuscan mainland. The slopes of the mountain are rendered even more beautiful by the flowering broom.

The Mediterranean scrub and the emerald green tonalities of the sea characterize the pleasant landscape of the gulf of Lacona. On the following pages: aspects of the nature and the enviroment of the splendid Gulf of Stella.

Lacona - The Gulf of Stella

Leaving Marina di Campo and heading in the direction of Capoliveri, the road, which at first runs along the coast, now runs down into one of the most spectacular areas of scenic and enviromental beauty, giving us panoramic views of extraordinary charm.

Lacona has a wide sandy shore, surrounded by the thick and shady pines, and looks out onto the gulf of the same name which lies between Capo di Fonza and Capo della Stella. This region has numerous camp sites and private residences, and is one of the most pleasant and "sun-kissed" beaches on the whole island. Its name could also account for the origin of the thin flat coastal stretch where the beach is situated: it seems to derive its name from the Latin *Lacuna* = lagoon, which however refers to an old coastal pond/pool, which has now dried up and has been drained. In order to try to make the surrounding plain fertile and tillable, a vast number of eucalyptus and tropical trees which are known to extract great quantities of water from the soil, thereby draining it, have been planted in the area. These trees also have the function of acting as a barrier to the violent sea breezes which plague the coast, and the trees and bushes that were planted here have quickly grown to become luxuriant, and therefore now give excellent shelter from the summer heat to tourists and campers alike.

The *gulf of Stella* is a wide inlet which lies between the cape of the same name and Capo Morocone. You are advised to leave your car at the beginning of the promontory which separates the two gulfs, so that you can more easily admire the spectacular views which can be seen from the gulf of Lacone and the gulf of Stella, within a beautiful framework of lush and exuberant Mediterranean scrub, which here has species typical of the southernmost latitudes. The coastal outline of the gulf of Stella, emphasised by little promontories, projections and romantic coves, gradually vanishes in the east in the direction of the beach of the Lido, which is near to Capoliveri.

Capoliveri

The small town has around 2,000 inhabitants and stands, in a pleasant and charming position, on the summit of a panoramic hill, in a area which is important because of the presence of several mines which are still worked even today. The urban structure has extremely interesting aspects: the houses are closely grouped together, so that they could be more easily defended. However another reason why the houses were grouped together in this way, was that by this method, the small area of flat surfaces could therefore be fully exploited. The streets are narrow, steep and paved with stones.

The centre of Capoliveri has always been inhabited even as far back as ancient times; its very name seems to derive from the Latin place-name, *Caput Liberi* = the mountain of Libero. The reference to this ancient Itallic divinity, who corresponds to Bacchus, god of wine, seems to be affirmed by the fact that as far back as the olden days (and maybe to a much greater extent than today) the slopes of Capoliveri have always been covered with vines which produce an excellent wine. Capoliveri enjoyed its greatest period in the XIVth century when it became the seat of the podesta (chief town of the Commune) of Pisa, which, with the power entrusted to it, ruled the whole of the island for six months: in those times the town also had a large port situated in the nearby gulf of Mola. After a long period of decline, in which it was incorporated (from an administrative point of view) with the neighbouring Commune of Porto Azzurro, it finally regained its autonomy in 1907.

The plan of the town clearly shows the characteristics of a medieval town; in particular we can see the unusual arrangement of the houses, which are arranged in a semicircle, and which re-echo the ancient perimeter of the walls, restructured and transformed so as to be more in keeping with the town buildings.

On the facing page: a picturesque glimpse of the roofs of Capoliveri. Above: a typical street in the centre of Capoliveri.

1

2

3

1. Panorama of Capoliveri; 2. The Santuary of the Madonna delle Grazie; 3. The restored bell-tower of the Parish Church dominates the roofs of Capoliveri. On the following pages: a view of the coasts of Elba as seen from the verdant Capo Perla.

In the vicinity of Capoliveri we find constructions which are quite interesting; near the cemetry one can see the ruins of the **Church of S. Michele**, which is in all probability a Romanesque-Pisan parish church dating back to the XIIth century. Particularly worth mentioning is the rear portion of the apse, scanned by parastades and decorated by a series of blind arches and small windows. According to ancient legend, Pope Gregorie XI. held a mass here, on his way back from Avignone to Rome.

The **Sanctuary of the Madonna delle Grazie** is a small construction of the XII. century, characterized by a pretty round cupola and a belltower with a globe in the masonry. The interior has a lacunar ceiling and painting of the XVIth century, believed to be the work of pupils of Raphael. Near the pleasant

and evocative Capo Perla, covered by a thick pine forest, which slopes down to the pleasant sickle-shaped inlet, where the vast sandy shore of *Straccoligno* opens out, is situated **Fort Focardo**. This was constructed by the Spanish in the second half of the XVIIth century, and has a powerful presence which is rendered by the huge walls which tower over the waters of the sea below. It was built to defend and control the main port of the island, Porto Azzurro; the fort is nowadays used as a lighthouse and therefore is run by the Navy.

The enchanting *Cala dell'Innamorata* should also be men-

Above: a view of the shore of Straccoligno, with Capo Perla in the background. On the facing page: two views of the golf courses in the locality of Acquabona.

1. A splendid view of the Cala dell'Innamorata which faces the Gemini Islands; 2. A view of the shore of the Innamorata; 3. The houses of the Innamorata stretch out along the foot of Mount Calamita.

tioned, which picturesquely opens out on the south eastern slopes of Mt. Calamita. The magnificent sandy shore is crowned by reliefs which are thickly covered by the unmistakable Mediterranean scrub. In this corner of exceeding beauty, characterised by the *Gemini Islands* two rocks which rise up out of the azzure waters of the Tyrrhene Sea, just off the promontory which lies to the south of the cove, one finds an abundance of Indian fig trees and agaves which confirm the presence of a warm sunny climate.

CONTENTS

Editing
Editing Studio - Pisa

Graphics and Lay-out
Bruno Farese, Stefania Forconi/Energia S.n.c. - Pisa

Translation
Rhiannon Lewis